1

ELECTRICITY

By
Emilie Dufresne

BookLife PUBLISHING

©2019
BookLife Publishing Ltd.
King's Lynn
Norfolk PE30 4LS

All rights reserved.
Printed in Malaysia.

A catalogue record for this book is available from the British Library.

ISBN: 978-1-78637-795-1

Written by:
Emilie Dufresne

Edited by:
Madeline Tyler

Designed by:
Gareth Liddington

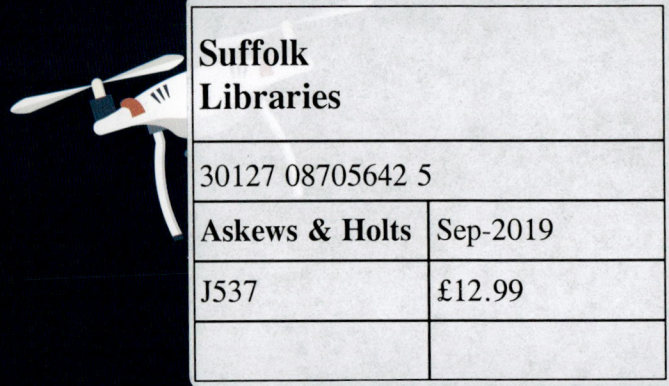

Suffolk Libraries	
30127 08705642 5	
Askews & Holts	Sep-2019
J537	£12.99

Photocredits:

Cover – GraphicsRF, matrioshka, d1sk, Janos Levente, Stock_VectorSale, Be.sign, lenoleum, 4 – Elventica, Made by Marko, 5 – Niwat signsamarn, 6 – fredrisher, Maksim M, ONYXprj, 8 – Washdog, 9 – Mark1987, Andriy A, 10 – Edilus, Creative Mood, IconBunny, 12 – Dinosoft Labs, petovarga, 14 – Natali Snailcat, 15 – Pretty Vectors, Roi and Roi, 18 – ironwool, grmarc, SThom, 19 – meliun, Enmaler, 20 – petovarga, 21 – Anatolir, Panda Vector, Marnikus.

Images are courtesy of Shutterstock.com. With thanks to Getty Images, Thinkstock Photo and iStockphoto.

All facts, statistics, web addresses and URLs in this book were verified as valid and accurate at time of writing.
No responsibility for any changes to external websites or references can be accepted by either the author or publisher.

Contents

Page 4 — What Is Electricity?
Page 6 — What Uses Electricity?
Page 8 — Batteries
Page 10 — Good and Bad Electricity
Page 12 — Building Circuits
Page 14 — Electric Animals
Page 16 — Lightning
Page 18 — Benjamin Franklin
Page 20 — Electric Cars
Page 22 — Static Comb Experiment
Page 24 — Glossary and Index

Words that look like <u>this</u> can be found in the glossary on page 24.

What Is Electricity?

Electricity is a type of <u>energy</u>. It can be used to power electrical items such as your TV, kettle and the lights in your house.

Kettle

Lights

Electricity is created when tiny <u>particles</u> called electrons move around.

Electricity can either be static or flowing. Static electricity is still, and flowing electricity moves in a <u>current</u>. Here are some examples of static electricity:

When a balloon sticks to your hair

Static shocks from metal objects

What Uses Electricity?

Nowadays we use electricity so much that it is easy to forget just how many things need electricity to work.

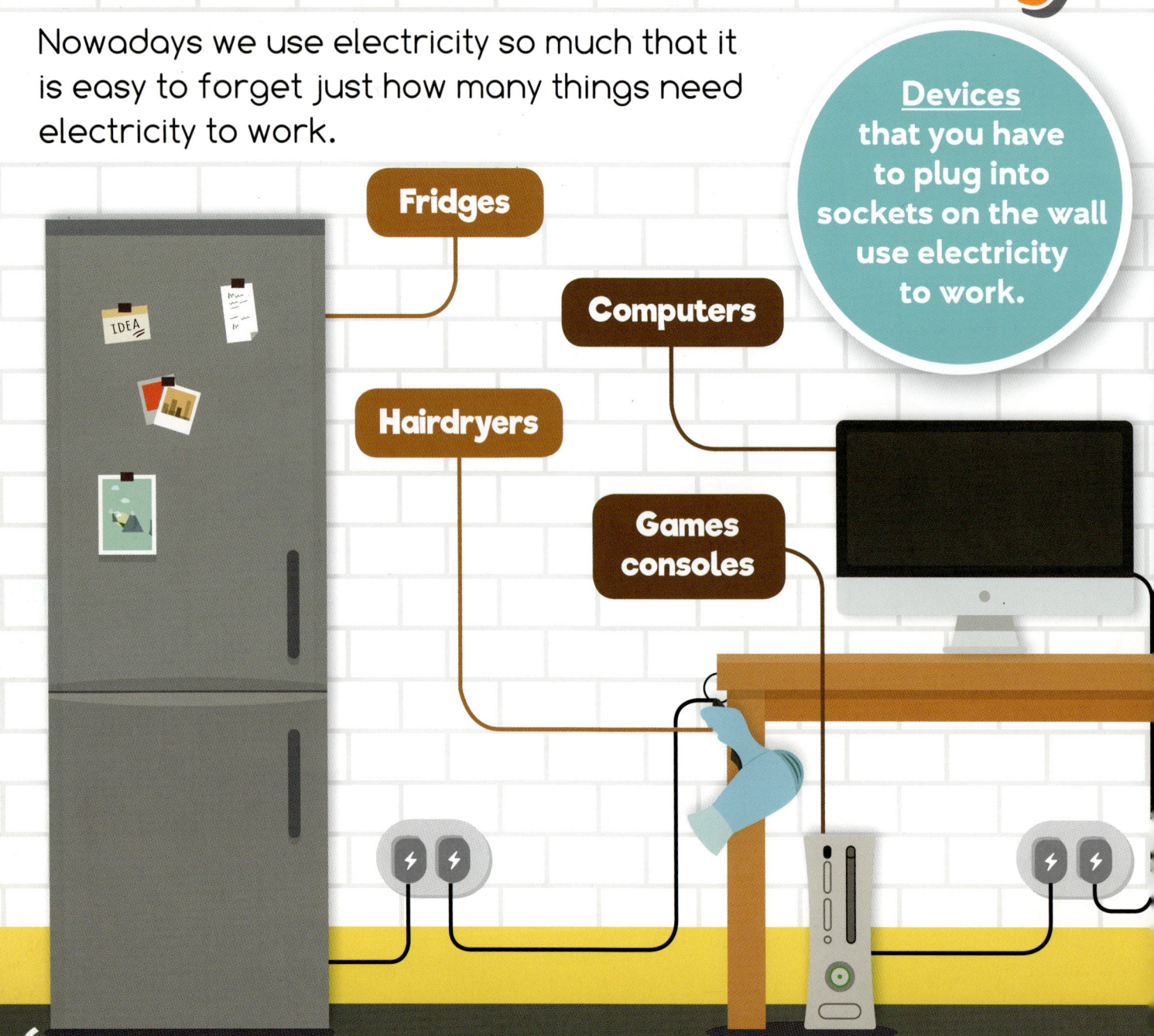

Fridges

Computers

Hairdryers

Games consoles

Devices that you have to plug into sockets on the wall use electricity to work.

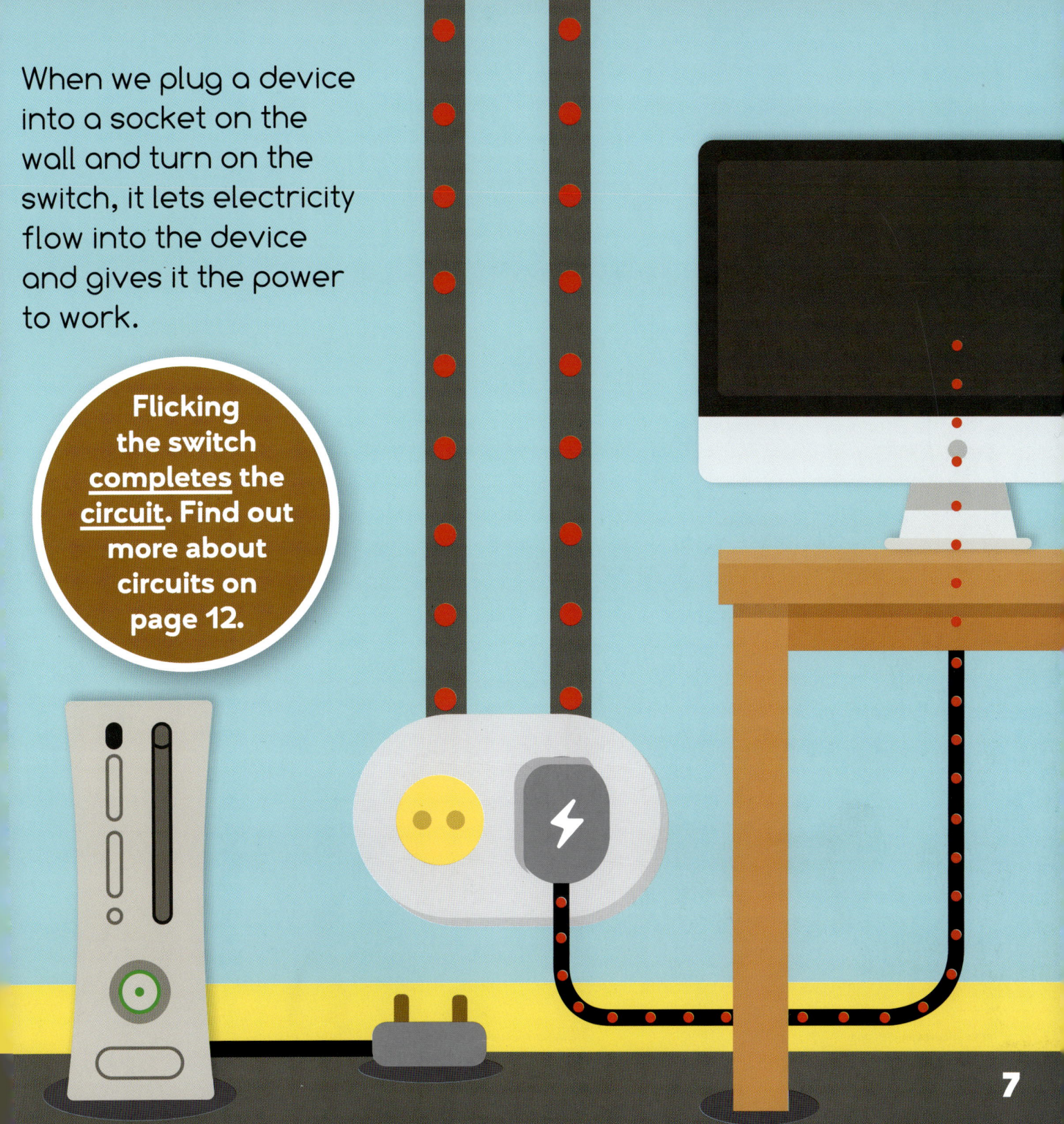

When we plug a device into a socket on the wall and turn on the switch, it lets electricity flow into the device and gives it the power to work.

Flicking the switch <u>completes</u> the <u>circuit</u>. Find out more about circuits on page 12.

Batteries

Some devices might need batteries. This means that they still use electricity but don't need to be plugged in to use them.

Batteries store energy, which is ready to be used whenever it is needed.

Full charge

Low charge

Some devices already have batteries inside them. These include laptops and mobile phones. You have to plug these devices in to charge the batteries.

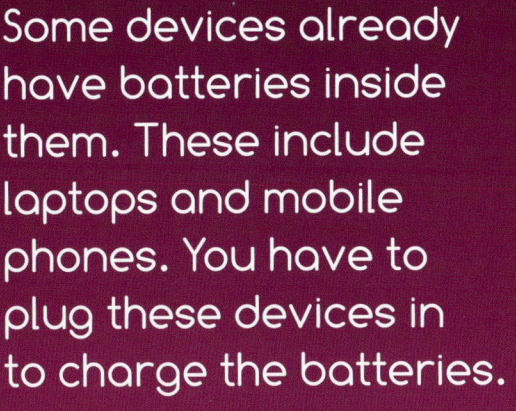

Devices such as your TV controller or a remote control car need batteries put in them to work.

Put batteries here

9

Good and Bad Electricity

There are lots of ways to make electricity. Some of these ways are better for our environment than others.

Wind power

Energy sources that are better for our environment are also known as green energy sources.

GREEN ENERGY SOURCES

Hydropower

Solar power

Energy sources that are bad for our environment are known as non-renewable energy sources.

Around three-quarters of electricity used is from bad electricity sources. Only a quarter comes from green energy sources.

NON RENEWABLE ENERGY SOURCES

Nuclear power

Coal

Oil

Building Circuits

Circuits give a current of electricity a set path to travel on. This makes sure that the electricity can be used to do something useful, such as making your lights work.

To make your own circuit you will need:

- A switch
- A lightbulb
- A power source
- Wires and crocodile clips

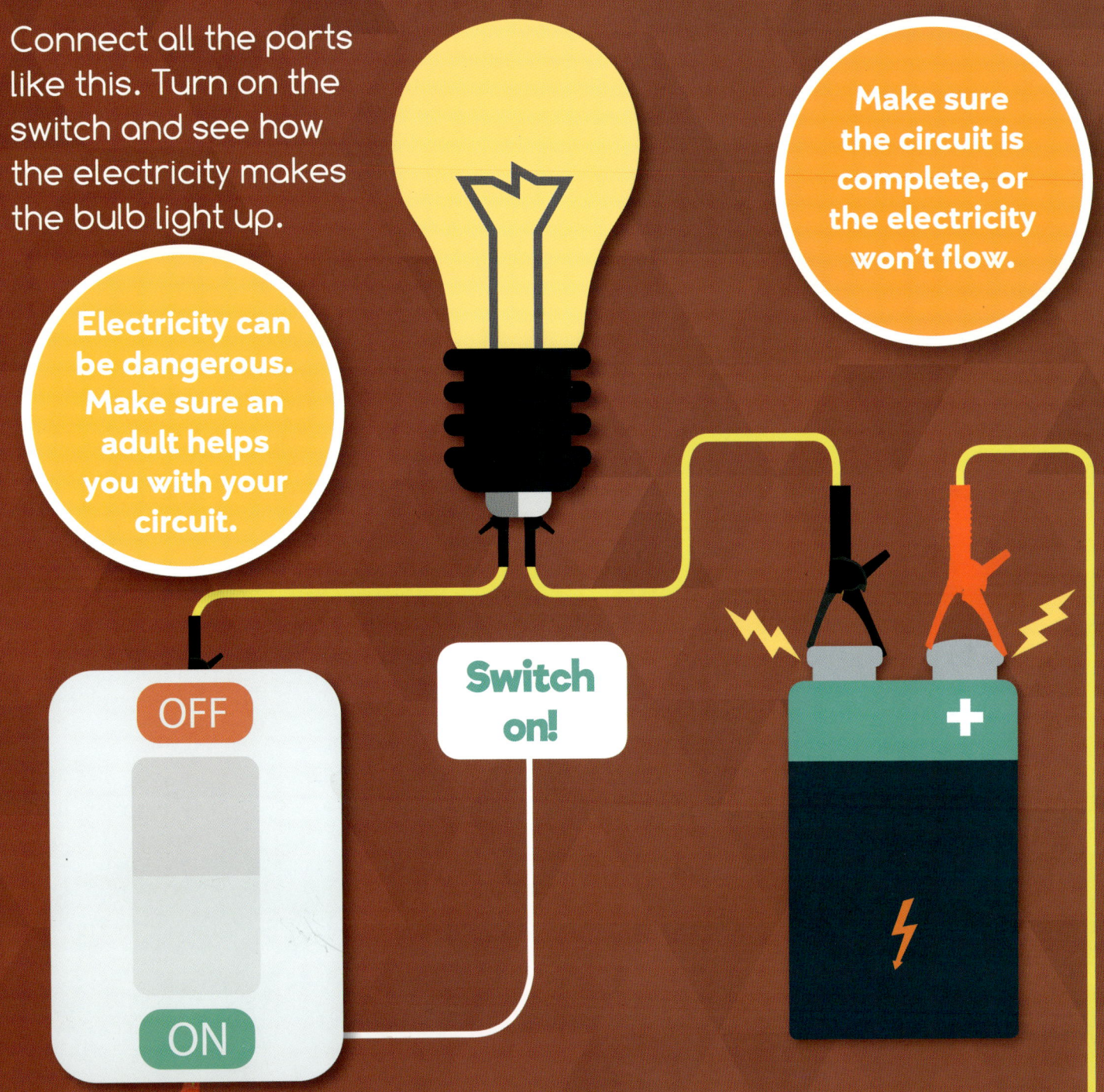

Electric Animals

Electric eels have a special power. Their cells can store energy like a battery does.

They can then use this electricity to attack their prey.

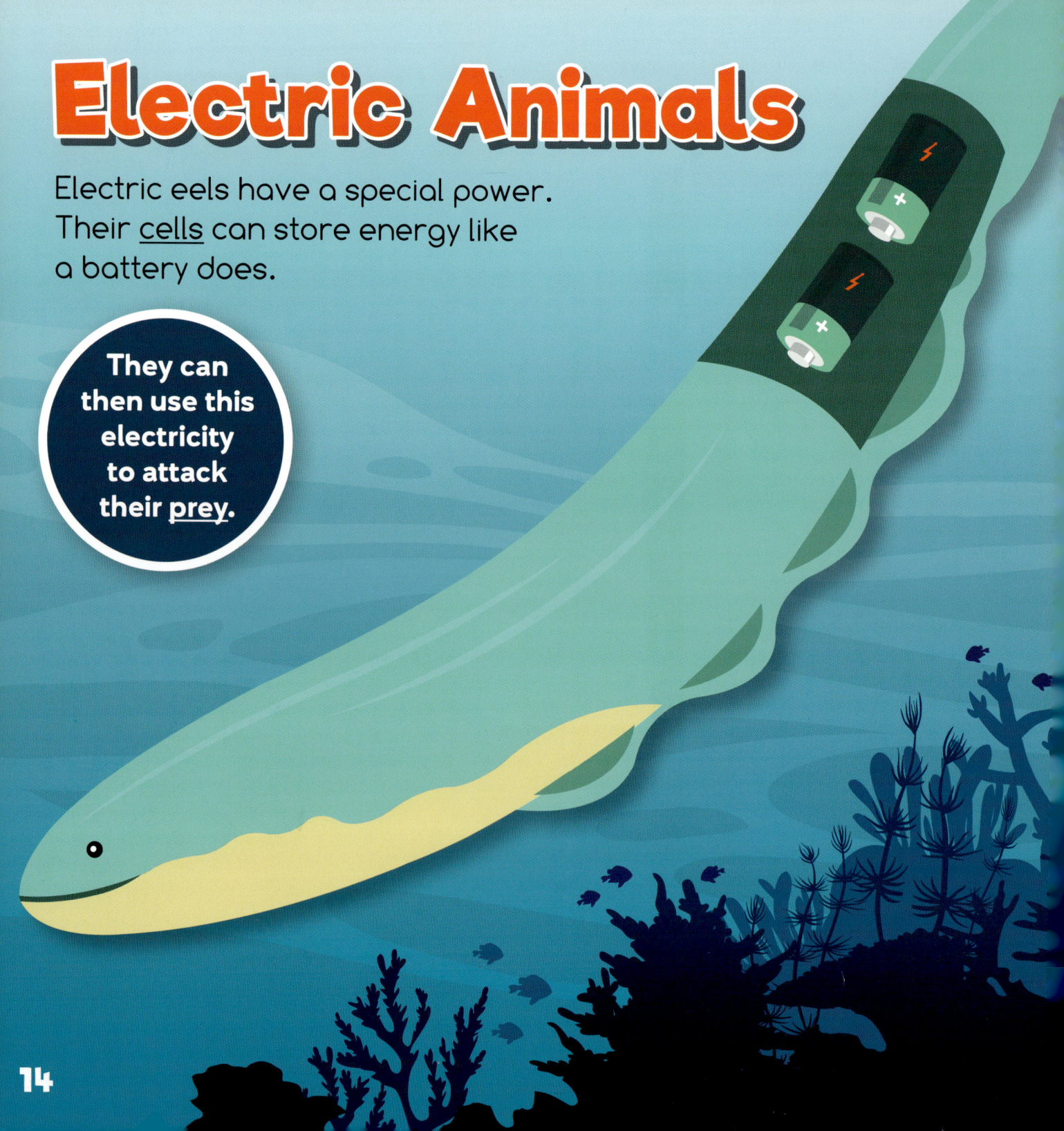

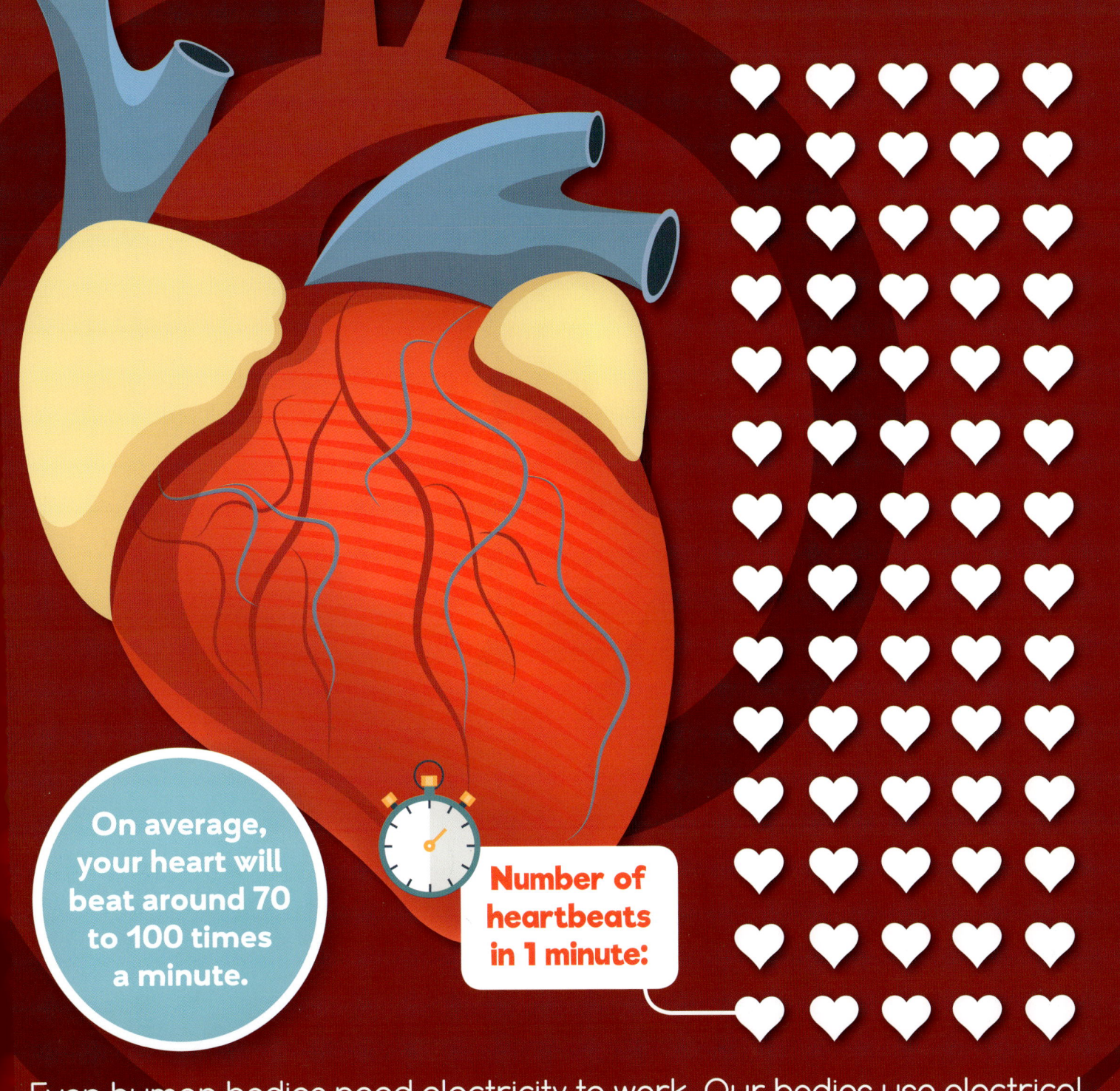

On average, your heart will beat around 70 to 100 times a minute.

Number of heartbeats in 1 minute:

Even human bodies need electricity to work. Our bodies use electrical messages to make our hearts pump blood around our bodies.

Lightning

Lightning is type of electrical current. It is created when particles in a cloud move around and make static electricity. This electricity finds a path from the sky to the ground.

> As lightning travels to the ground, it creates a very hot, giant spark.

Flash!   **1 second**   **2 seconds**   **3 seconds**

Light travels much faster than sound. You will see the lightning spark before hearing the thunder. After you see the lightning spark, count in seconds until you hear the thunder.

For every three seconds you count, the thunderstorm is one kilometre away.

Benjamin Franklin

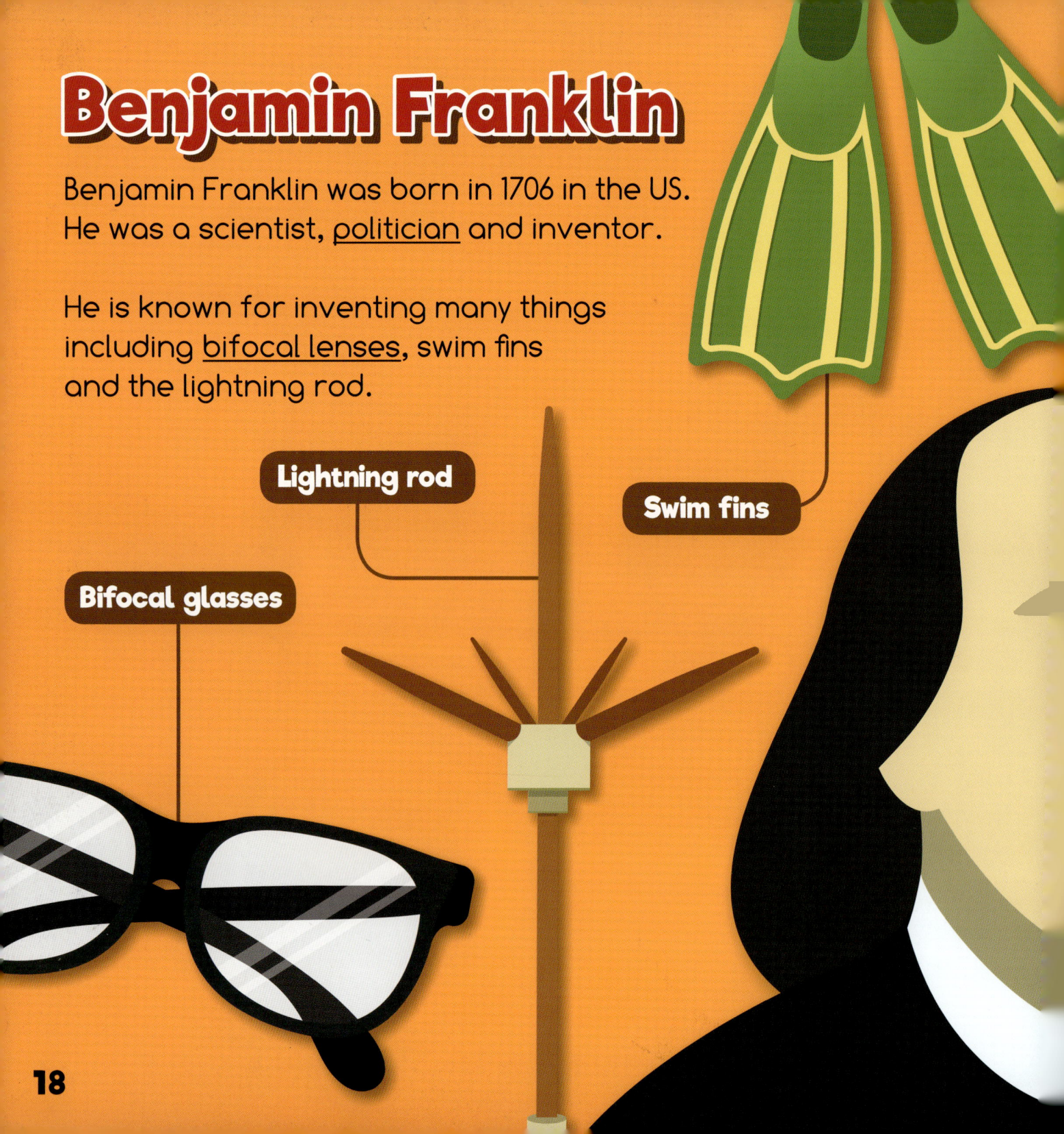

Benjamin Franklin was born in 1706 in the US. He was a scientist, <u>politician</u> and inventor.

He is known for inventing many things including <u>bifocal lenses</u>, swim fins and the lightning rod.

Lightning rod

Swim fins

Bifocal glasses

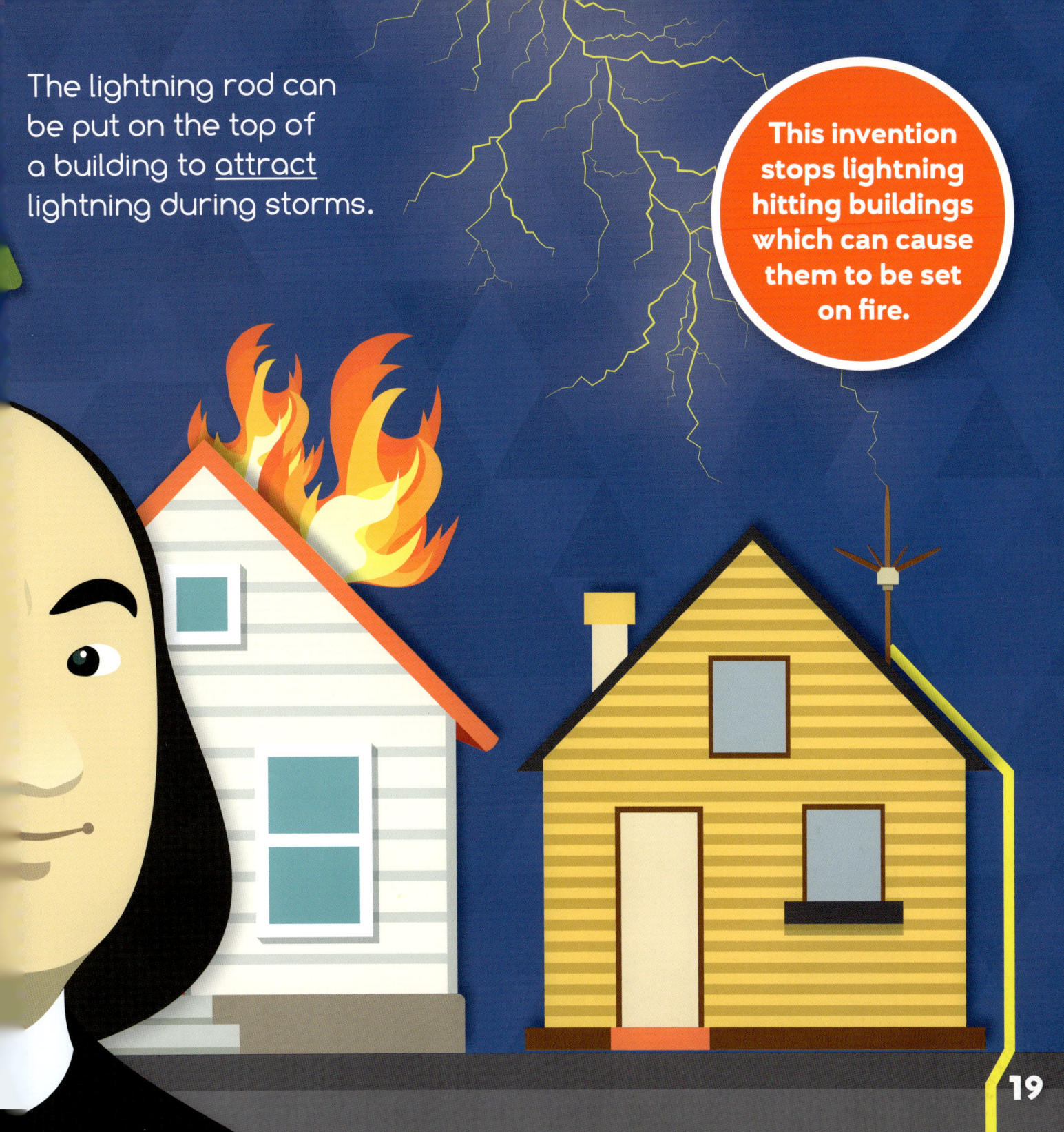

Electric Cars

Electric cars have been around for over 100 years. Now they can be used instead of cars that run on fuel.

This can be better for the environment as long as the electricity comes from a green electricity source.

ELECTRIC CARS

Electric cars are becoming more popular. However, electric cars still make up fewer than 1 percent of all cars on the road.

The more electric cars we use, the better it could be for the environment.

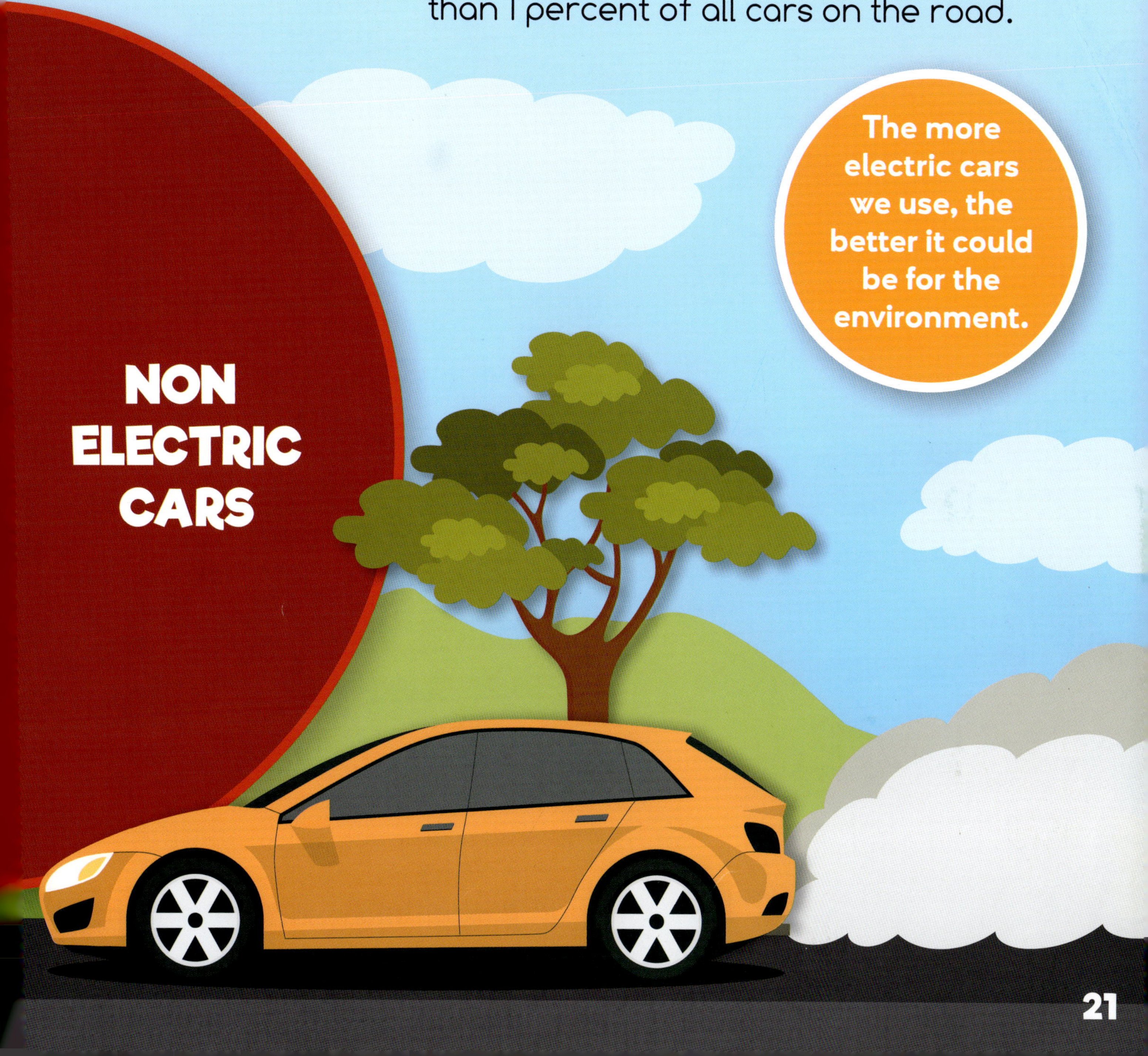

NON ELECTRIC CARS

Static Comb Experiment

It's time to experiment!
You will need:

- A plastic comb
- A tap
- A woollen jumper

STEP 1
Rub the comb on your jumper in the same direction for 30 seconds.

STEP 2
Turn on the tap so that it has a slow, steady stream of water.

STEP 3
Hold the comb near to the water, but not touching the water.

The water should be attracted to, and bend towards, the static electricity built up by the comb.

What happened during your experiment?

23

Glossary

attract	pull towards
bifocal lenses	used in bifocal glasses: glasses that have two sections of lenses, one for looking at near things and one for looking at things that are far away
cells	the basic building blocks of all living things
circuit	a path for electric currents to move around
completes	makes something whole and unbroken
current	a movement or flow of something in one direction
devices	machines or inventions made to do something
energy	a type of power, such as electricity or heat, that can be used for a purpose
environment	the natural world around us
particles	tiny things that are too small to see, which make up everything
politician	a person involved with politics
prey	animals that are eaten by other animals for food

Index

batteries 8-9, 14
circuits 7, 12-13
current 5, 12-13
devices 6-9
energy 4, 8, 10-11, 14
experiments 22-23

Franklin, Benjamin 18
lightning 16-19
sparks 16-17
static 5, 16, 22-23
switches 7, 12-13
thunder 17